ARE YOU SMARTER THAN A 5TH GRADER?

TEST YOUR SMARTS!

SCIENCE

by Kris Hirschmann
and Ryan Herndon

Thanks to Mark Burnett Productions,
especially Mark Burnett, Barry Poznick, John Stevens,
Sue Guercioni, Amanda Harrell, and Laura Ambriz

SCHOLASTIC INC.
New York Toronto London Auckland Sydney
Mexico City New Delhi Hong Kong Buenos Aires

SCHOLASTIC

The publisher would like to thank the following for their kind permission to use their photographs in this book:

5 Camel © Ana Vasileva/Shutterstock; 6 *Stegosaurus* © Fotoadamczyk/Shutterstock; 7 Spider, 76 Microscope © StillFx/Shutterstock; 8 Bear © Suzann Julien/iStockphoto; 9 Ladybugs © Oktay Ortakcioglu/iStockphoto; 9 Kangaroo, 19 Emu, 35 Lion © Eric Isselee/Shutterstock; 10 Octopus art, 35 Fish art © Sabri Deniz Kizil/Shutterstock; 11 Penguin art © Alan Sprong/Shutterstock, Astronaut © Glushkova Olga Valdimirovna/Shutterstock; 12, 36, 53 Planets, 51 Comet © Nat Ulrich/Shutterstock; 12 Earth © Roslen Mack/Shutterstock; 13 Carrot © Ackab Photography/Shutterstock; 14 Human arm skeleton, 69 Bacteria © Sebastian Kaulitzki/Shutterstock; 14 Caduceus © Robertas/Shutterstock; 17, 31, 45 Pencil © Stetom/Shutterstock; 17, 31, 61 Pencil Sharpener © SNR/Shutterstock; 19 Mosquito © Ismael Montero Verdu/Shutterstock, Ant © Markov/Shutterstock; 20 Crocodile © Aleynikov Pavel/Shutterstock, Chimp art © Betamax/Shutterstock; 21 Humpback whale art © Oscar F. Chuyn/Shutterstock, Dragonfly © Saied Shahin Kiya/Shutterstock; 22 Sea anemone © David McKee/Shutterstock; 25 Raindrop art © WitchEra/Shutterstock; 26 Cloud art © Deedl/Shutterstock; 27 Plant, Root © Procurator/Shutterstock; 28 Heart rate © Marie Cloke/Shutterstock; 33 Butterfly © Cardiae/Shutterstock, World map art © Adrian Grosu/Shutterstock; 34 Sea horse © Kalim/Shutterstock, Orca © Christian Musat/Shutterstock; 36 Sun art © Jennifer Johnson, BlueCherry Graphics/Shutterstock; 37 Galaxy © Stephen Girimont/Shutterstock; 39 Gemstones © Nagib/Shutterstock; 40 Iceberg © Jartur Snorrason/Shutterstock; 42 Cocoa beans © Howard Sandler/Shutterstock, Bird art © Myper/Shutterstock; 43 Leaves, 67 Earth and moon © Paul Paladin/Shutterstock; 43 Cactus desert © Ozger Aybike Sarikay/Shutterstock; 44 Skeleton © Shamzam/Shutterstock; 45, 61 Erasers © Mariano N. Ruiz/Shutterstock; 49 Bee, 65 Insects art © Robert Adrian Hillman/Shutterstock; 50 Butterflies © Mirjana Banjac/Shutterstock; 52 Moon phases © Albo003/Shutterstock; 53 Lightening © Din/Shutterstock; 54 Aurora © Roman Krochuk/Shutterstock; 55 Tree © Pkruger/Shutterstock; 56 Potted plant © Elena Butinova/Shutterstock; 57 Animal skeleton art © Potapov Alexander/Shutterstock; 59 Dreamer © Phil Date/Shutterstock; 63 Ruler © PeppPic/Shutterstock; 65 Elephants © Ted Nad/Shutterstock; 66 Astronaut © Pxlar8/Shutterstock; 70 Soccer ball, Water © PhotoCreate/Shutterstock; 71 *T. rex* art © Jenny Horne/Shutterstock; 73 Periodic table © Scott Rothstein/Shutterstock; 74 Volcano © Julien Grondin/Shutterstock; 75 Tsunami © Mana Photo/Shutterstock.

ISBN-13: 978-0-545-12041-8
ISBN-10: 0-545-12041-1

Designed by Michelle Martinez
Photo researched by Michelle Martinez and Els Rijper

12 11 10 9 8 7 6 5 4 3 2 1   9 10 11 12 13 14/0

Printed in the U.S.A.
First printing, February 2009

SCIENCE

SMARTY ALERT

Lights . . . Camera . . . ACTION!
Since its debut in 2007, the hit game show
"Are You Smarter Than A 5th Grader?"
has proven that most adults *did* forget
their grade-school lessons. During the
show's first two seasons, not one
contestant took home the $1,000,000
grand prize.

Think you can do better? Here's your
chance to test your smarts in the subject of
SCIENCE. Will you ace this test or flunk
out? Grab a pencil, turn the page, and find
out if you're smarter than a 5th grader!

1ST Grade

STARTING WITH THE BASICS

First grade is fun! In this year,
kids concentrate on building a good foundation
of science knowledge. It's all about basic facts —
simple stuff that everyone needs to know to
understand the world around us. Yes, we said simple.
These questions are easy, and they're supposed to be.
But don't get too comfortable. TV contestants
have flunked out on first-grade questions.
Let's see if *you* can make the grade!

ANIMAL SCIENCE

1. A doe is the female of which of the following animals?
   a) Dog
   b) Deer
   c) Horse

2. **True or False?** A camel's hump is primarily used to hold water.

3. Which is the largest species of cat?
   a) Tiger
   b) Puma
   c) Jaguar

4. **True or False?** Female goats can produce milk.

5. Which of the following animals is NOT native to the African savanna?
   a) Giraffe
   b) Lion
   c) Brown bear

6. **True or False?** A typical male moose sheds its antlers every year.

7. **True or False?** All birds are mammals.

8. **True or False?** This picture is an image of a *Tyrannosaurus rex*.

7x7=49   AaBbCcDdEe

9. **True or False?** Every adult rhinoceros has exactly one horn.

10. A group of wolves is called a pack. What do we call a group of lions?
a) Prestige
b) Pride
c) Pack

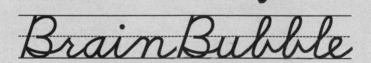

11. **True or False?**
A spider is an insect.

Brain Bubble

Name That Group

Most animal groups have names. Some, like a **flock** of birds or a **school** of fish, are familiar to many. Other names are not as well known. How about a **murder** of crows, an **exaltation** of larks, or a **knot** of toads? All of these group names are real . . . and really strange, too!

12. What land mammal runs the fastest?

13. **True or False?** Komodo dragons are extinct.

14. **True or False?** Walruses are native to the Arctic.

15. What is the largest species of bear?

16. An elephant's tusks are made primarily of what material?
a) Enamel
b) Bone marrow
c) Ivory

17. True or False? All ladybugs are female.

18. By definition, the word "bovine" refers to which of the following animals?
a) Cow
b) Pig
c) Dog

19. True or False? All adult kangaroos have pouches.

20. **True or False?** Africa is the only continent where elephants exist naturally in the wild.

21. **True or False?** The toucan is a freshwater fish.

22. How many arms does a typical octopus have?

Brain Bubble

Walking Heads

Octopuses and their relatives, the squids, nautiluses, and cuttlefish, are known as **cephalopods**. This word means "head-footed." It's no mystery how the group got this name. In all cephalopods, the "legs" (which are actually called arms or sometimes tentacles) are connected directly to the head.

7×7=49   AaBbCcDdEe

23. **True or False?** In the wild, polar bears typically feed on penguins.

24. How many horns did the *Triceratops* dinosaur have on its head?

25. What gemstone is formed inside mollusks such as oysters?

ASTRONOMY

26. The Sun is primarily made up of which substance?
a) Gas
b) Molten metal
c) Rock

27. What is the only planet in our solar system that people have walked on?

AaBbCcDdEe

28. **True or False?** You can see the planet Saturn with the naked eye.

29. What star is closest to the Earth?

30. What object in our solar system is the primary source of solar power on Earth?

EARTH SCIENCE

31. **True or False?** Lightning is a form of precipitation.

32. By definition, what does a weathervane measure?
a) Rainfall
b) Wind direction
c) Air temperature

7x7=49   AaBbccDdEe

NATURE

33. Which of the following foods has seeds inside?
a) Orange
b) Potato
c) Carrot

34. **True or False?** All carrots are orange in color.

35. Rice is what type of food?
a) Fruit
b) Grain
c) Vegetable

36. The food known as pork comes from what animal?

37. We exhale what gas that plants need in order to live?

HEALTH

38. **True or False?** The esophagus is a passageway that connects the mouth to the nose.

39. What is the name of the joint in the human body that connects the hand to the forearm?

40. If you bump your "funny bone," what joint did you hit?

Brain Benders

EXTRA CREDIT

41. In the Northern Hemisphere, summer ends in which month?

42. The period of Daylight Saving Time includes which two of the four seasons in their entirety?

Are you Smarter Than a 5th Grader

$6 \times 6 = 36$
$7 \times 7 = 49$

ANIMAL SCIENCE

1. **b. Deer**. Female deer are called does, and males are called bucks.

2. **False**. A camel's hump primarily holds fat.

3. **a. Tiger**. Pumas and jaguars are smaller.

4. **True**. Goats are mammals, and all female mammals produce milk.

5. **c. Brown bear**. This species is native to Europe, Asia, and North America.

6. **True**. A male moose grows new antlers each time it loses a pair.

7. **False**. Unlike birds, mammals have body hair and give birth to live young.

8. **False**. The picture shows a *Stegosaurus*, which lived during the same period as *T. rex*.

9. **False**. Some, but not all, rhinoceroses have two horns.

10. **b. Pride**. The members of a pride live and hunt together.

11. **False**. Spiders, ticks, and scorpions are arachnids.

12. **Cheetah**. The fastest land mammal has been clocked at speeds up to 71 miles per hour.

13. **False**. Komodo dragons, the world's largest lizards, still roam wild on Komodo Island in Indonesia.

14. **True**. These huge, seal-like animals are found in and near Arctic seas.

15. **Polar Bear**. The largest bear species lives in the Arctic.

16. **c. Ivory**. A unique type of dentin, ivory is the main material found in teeth.

17. **False**. Despite their name, ladybugs can be either male or female.

18. **a. Cow**. Cowlike animals such as bison, water buffaloes, and yaks are also referred to as bovines.

19. **False.** Only female kangaroos have pouches.

20. **False**. Elephants also occur naturally in Asia.

21. **False**. The toucan is a type of bird.

22. **Eight**. Octopuses use their arms for crawling and catching food.

23. **False**. Polar bears prefer seals above all other food.

24. **Three**. *Triceratops* had one horn on its nose and two growing out of its forehead.

25. **Pearl**. Oysters make pearls by coating bits of foreign matter with a shiny material called nacre.

ASTRONOMY

26. a. Gas. Hydrogen and helium make up almost all of the Sun's mass.

27. Earth. People also have walked on the Moon, but the Moon is not classified as a planet.

28. True. Saturn is easily visible at night. It looks like a non-twinkling point of light.

29. The Sun. The next closest star, Proxima Centauri, is about 4.2 million light-years away.

30. The Sun. This star is the source of virtually all of the energy on Earth.

EARTH SCIENCE

31. False. Lightning is a form of electricity.

32. b. Wind direction. A weather-vane spins freely to point straight into the blowing wind.

NATURE

33. a. Orange. Potatoes and carrots are seedless.

34. False. White, yellow, and purple carrots also exist.

35. b. Grain. Rice is a cereal grain of the grass family.

36. Pig. Bacon and ham are also pig products.

37. Carbon dioxide. Plants use carbon dioxide and water to turn sunlight into energy.

HEALTH

38. False. The esophagus connects the mouth to the stomach.

39. Wrist. This joint lets the hand bend up and down and side to side.

40. Elbow. The ulnar nerve produces a "tingly" feeling if the elbow is hit.

BRAIN BENDERS

41. September. In the United States, summer officially runs from June 20 to September 20.

42. Spring and summer. In the United States, Daylight Saving Time runs from the second Sunday in March until the first Sunday in November.

Did you
☐ pass or
☐ fail?

17

2ND Grade

PICKING UP THE PACE

Congratulations! You have a whole year of grade school under your belt. Now you're ready to tackle second grade, where the kids are a little smarter and the questions are a little tougher. To succeed at this level, you'll need to pick up the pace — shifting from first gear into second. Child's play, you say? Second-grade questions have stumped plenty of grown-up contestants. Let's see how well you do when the rubber hits the road!

ANIMAL SCIENCE

1. What gender of mosquitoes bites humans?

2. **True or False?** Chickens are cold-blooded animals.

3. Cows exist in herds, while ants live in groups called what?
   a) Colonies
   b) Communities
   c) Clusters

4. **True or False?**
   The emu is a flightless bird.

AaBbCcDdEe

5. **True or False?** All crocodiles are herbivores.

6. What species of land animal is the closest surviving relative of the extinct woolly mammoth?

7. The chimpanzee's native habitat is on what continent?

8. The female of which animal species is called an ewe?

7x7=49 AaBbCcDdEe

9. How many legs does a butterfly have?

10. True or False?
The hump-
back whale is
cold-blooded.

11. Which of the following is an insect body part?
a) Lorax
b) Thorax
c) Syntax

12. The alpaca is a species of animal in what family?
a) Camel
b) Lizard
c) Dog

AaBbCcDdEe

13. **True or False?** Butterflies have teeth to bite and chew their food.

14. **True or False?** Giant pandas hibernate.

15. **True or False?** There are no species of fish that are immune to the poison of a sea anemone.

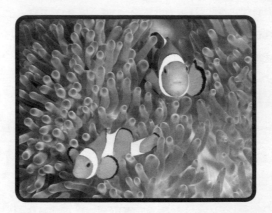

16. A paleontologist is a scientist who finds and studies:
    a. Living animals
    b. Living plants
    c. Fossils

7x7=49   AaBbCcDdEe

17. What living bird lays the biggest eggs?

18. **True or False?** The wolverine is a member of the canine family.

19. Which of the following is a venomous snake?
a) Python
b) Cobra
c) Anaconda

Brain Bubble

Poison vs. Venom

There's a difference between poisonous and venomous animals. Snakes and other venomous creatures deliberately inject toxins into their victims, usually by biting or stinging. Poisonous creatures carry toxins in or on their bodies, but they won't make you sick unless you touch them or eat them.

AaBbCcDdEe

ASTRONOMY

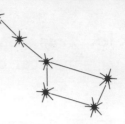

20. What constellation contains the Big Dipper?

21. Which planet is typically the brightest in the night sky?

22. True or False? Meteor showers can occur when the Earth passes through the dust of a comet's tail.

23. The planet Earth is located in what galaxy?

24. True or False? The planet Jupiter has a larger mass than Earth.

7x7=49   AaBbccDdEe

25. The oceans' tides are caused mainly by the gravitational pull between the Earth and what heavenly body?

26. True or False? The Moon does not produce its own light.

EARTH SCIENCE

27. True or False? All snowflakes are 10-sided geometric figures.

28. A long period with less-than-expected rainfall is called a:
a) Flood
b) Drought
c) Thirst

29. About how many hours does it take for the Earth to spin one full time on its axis?

AaBbCcDdEe

30. **True or False?** A river's place of origin is its mouth.

31. **True or False?** Stratus clouds are typically at a higher altitude than cirrus clouds.

32. A manmade lake created for the purpose of storing water is called what?
a) Channel
b) Reservoir
c) Isthmus

Brain Bubble

One Big Lake

One of the largest manmade lakes in the United States is called Lake Mead. Stretching across parts of Nevada and Arizona, this lake formed when the Hoover Dam was built across the Colorado River. It is 115 miles long and holds over 10 trillion gallons of water.

7x7=49   AaBbCcDdEe

33. **True or False?** Almonds grow on trees.

34. **True or False?** Plants are not part of the food chain.

35. Which part of a plant collects nutrients from the soil?
a) Roots
b) Stem
c) Leaves

36. **True or False?** When a seed gets the right amount of water and warmth, it may start to germinate.

HEALTH

37. Which of the five senses is directly related to the olfactory system?

38. The process of pasteurization was developed from the work of which French scientist born in 1822?

39. Your skull surrounds and protects which of the following organs?
a) Heart
b) Stomach
c) Brain

40. **True or False?** During exercise, your heart rate slows down.

41. What is the name of the liquid in the human mouth that starts to break down food?

Brain Benders

EXTRA CREDIT

42. In the Northern Hemisphere, the summer solstice occurs in what month?

43. What state of matter is ice?
a) Solid
b) Gas
c) Liquid

Are you Smarter Than a 5th Grader

6×6=36
7×7=49

ANIMAL SCIENCE

1. **Female**. Male mosquitoes feed on plant nectar.

2. **False**. All birds are warm-blooded.

3. **a. Colonies**. Some ant colonies have millions of members.

4. **True**. The emu's wings are much too tiny to lift this big bird into the air.

5. **False**. Crocodiles are carnivores (meat-eaters), not herbivores (plant-eaters).

6. **The elephant**. Woolly mammoths probably acted a lot like their modern relatives.

7. **Africa**. Chimpanzees are found in West and Central Africa.

8. **Sheep**. Male sheep are called rams.

9. **Six**. Like all insects, butterflies have six legs.

10. **False**. Humpback whales are marine mammals, and like all mammals, they are warm-blooded.

11. **b. Thorax**. The head and the abdomen make up the other two parts of an insect's three-segment body.

12. **a. Camel**. The alpaca is a domesticated species of South American camelid.

13. **False**. Butterflies suck nectar through a strawlike proboscis.

14. **False**. Giant pandas spend a lot of time sleeping, but none in true hibernation.

15. **False**. The clownfish develops an immunity to the sea anemone's poison.

16. **c. Fossils**.

17. **Ostrich**. This living bird lays the biggest bird eggs.

18. **False**. Wolverines are most closely related to weasels.

19. **b. Cobra**. Pythons and anacondas are not venomous.

ASTRONOMY

20. **Ursa Major**. This constellation contains the seven brightest stars known as the Big Dipper.

21. **Venus**. Other than the Moon, this planet is the brightest object in the night sky.

22. **True**. Specks of dust turn into meteors when they hit the Earth's atmosphere.

23. **The Milky Way**. Our entire solar system is part of this galaxy.

24. **True**. Jupiter is more than 300 times heavier than Earth.

25. **The Moon**. Its gravitational pull has a powerful effect on the Earth's seas.

26. **True**. The Moon reflects light from the Sun.

EARTH SCIENCE

27. **False**. Snowflakes have six sides, or "arms."

28. **b. Drought**.

29. **24 hours**. This period is known as a day.

30. **False**. The mouth is the end of the river. The origin is called the source.

31. **False**. Stratus clouds form low layers. Cirrus clouds form high in the atmosphere.

32. **b. Reservoir**. These are usually made by building dams across rivers or streams.

NATURE

33. **True**. The fruits known as almonds are the seeds of the almond tree.

34. **False**. Plants are an extremely important part of the food chain.

35. **a. Roots**. The roots also anchor the plant.

36. **True**. The word "germinate" means "grow."

HEALTH

37. **Smell**. The word "olfactory" means "having to do with the sense of smell."

38. **Louis Pasteur**. This scientist grew up in the French town of Arbois.

39. **c. Brain**. The heart and the stomach are in the trunk of the body.

40. **False**. Your heart rate speeds up when you exercise.

41. **Saliva**. This liquid is sometimes called spit.

BRAIN BENDERS

42. **June**. The summer solstice occurs on June 20 or 21 each year.

43. **a. Solid**. In its liquid state, ice is called water. In its gas state, it is called water vapor.

Did you
☐ pass or
☐ fail?

3RD Grade

HALFWAY THERE

Third grade is a milestone! This year marks the halfway point between the first and fifth grades. Your teachers think you're ready to dive a little deeper into the science pool and learn some harder facts and concepts. Are you ready to go "swimming"? Test yourself with the third-grade science questions in this chapter. Only the smartest students will stay afloat!

ANIMAL SCIENCE

1. What is the last stage that a butterfly goes
   through before it becomes an adult?
   a) Egg
   b) Pupa
   c) Larva

2. **True or False?** The
   Alaskan malamute is
   a species of fish.

3. A giant panda's natural
   habitat is on what continent?

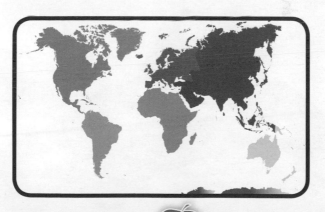

AaBbCcDdEe

4. Which of these animals
is a mammal?
a) Sea horse
b) Sea lion
c) Sea urchin

5. In terms of average weight,
what is the largest species of
snake in the world?

6. A drake is an adult male of
what species of bird?

7. True or False? The Orca is a type of
dolphin.

7x7=49   AaBbCcDdEe

8. **True or False?**
Only male lions
have manes.

9. **True or False?**
Polar bears have
black skin.

10. In fish, what is the name of the body
part that collects oxygen from the
water?

11. **True or False?** All fish lay eggs.

ASTRONOMY

12. **True or False?** Light is the only thing that can escape a black hole.

13. What is another name for the North Star?
a) Alpha Centauri
b) Polaris
c) Sirius

14. On which planet would a person weigh the most?
a) Mercury
b) Saturn
c) Jupiter

15. **True or False?** Earth is more than 50 million miles from the Sun.

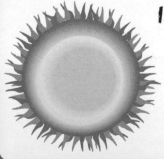

16. **True or False?** You would weigh more on the Moon than you do on Earth.

17. What planet is the second closest to the Sun?

18. **True or False?** The Milky Way galaxy contains more than one billion stars.

Brain Bubble

Billions and Billions of Galaxies

How many galaxies are out there? No one knows for sure, but it's A LOT! Until the early 1990s, there were thought to be about 10 billion galaxies in the universe. Now, thanks to better telescopes, scientists estimate that there are at least 50 to 100 billion galaxies in addition to the Milky Way.

19. Of the following, which kind of star is the hottest?
    a) Yellow star
    b) Blue giant
    c) Red dwarf

20. **True or False?** The Sun is the only star in our solar system.

21. Sometimes the Moon's shadow falls on the Earth's surface. This event is called a:
    a) Lunar eclipse
    b) Solar eclipse
    c) Planetary eclipse

EARTH SCIENCE

22. Granite is an example of what type of rock?
    a) Igneous
    b) Sedimentary
    c) Metamorphic

23. **True or False?** A tributary is a large river that flows into a smaller river.

24. **True or False?** More water vapor is held in cool air than in warm air.

25. **True or False?** Faint sunlight reaches the deepest parts of the ocean.

26. Gemstones are a type of:
    a) Rock
    b) Mineral
    c) Glass

AaBbCcDdEe

27. Name the three layers of the Earth.

28. There are three groups of rocks. Which of the following is not one of the three?
a) Sedimentary
b) Metamorphic
c) Obsidian

29. Which word describes a fairly flat area on the Earth's surface?
a) Plain
b) Valley
c) Barrier

30. In some places, huge sheets of ice flow across the Earth's surface. What are these ice sheets called?

31. Is the melted rock that reaches the Earth's surface called lava or magma?

32. About what percentage of the Earth's surface is covered by water?
a) 60%
b) 70%
c) 80%

33. From highest to lowest, put the layers of the Earth's atmosphere in order: mesosphere, stratosphere, thermosphere, troposphere.

NATURE

34. Fuji and Gala are both varieties of what fruit?

35. **True or False?**
Cocoa beans,
from which
chocolate is made,
originated in Asia.

36. **True or False?** All species of elm trees
are native to North America.

37. Which of the following is not a part of a
seed?
a) Seedling
b) Seed coat
c) Taproot

38. **True or False?**
Animals often
carry seeds
from one place
to another.

7x7=49   AaBbCcDdEe

39. Trees that lose and regrow their leaves each year are called:
a) Coniferous
b) Deciduous
c) Evergreens

40. **True or False?** It is much too dry for plants and animals to survive in most deserts.

Brain Bubble

A Hot Topic

People usually think of intense heat when they hear the word "desert." Some deserts are, indeed, extremely hot. But others, like the Antarctic, are freezing cold. Why? Deserts are defined by dryness, not temperature. To qualify as a desert, an area must receive no more than 10 inches of rainfall per year.

AaBbCcDdEe

HEALTH

41. The typical human body contains how many pairs of ribs?

42. What is the name of the largest bone in the human body?

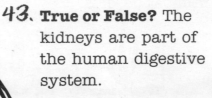

43. **True or False?** The kidneys are part of the human digestive system.

44. How many bones are in the typical adult human's body?
a) 206
b) 306
c) 406

AaBbCcDdEe

7x7=49

Brain Benders

EXTRA CREDIT

45. True or False? Standard pencil lead does not actually contain the element lead.

46. What are the three primary colors of light?

6x6=36
7x7=49

ANIMAL SCIENCE

1. **b. Pupa**. Butterflies start out as eggs, which hatch into larvae, which become pupae, which become adults.

2. **False**. The malamute is a species of dog.

3. **Asia**. Wild giant pandas are found only in China.

4. **b. Sea lion**. Sea horses are fish, and sea urchins are echinoderms.

5. **Anaconda**. It is the heaviest snake of the boa family.

6. **Duck**. Adult female ducks are called hens.

7. **True**. Although Orcas are nicknamed "killer whales," they are actually dolphins, not whales.

8. **True**. Female lions do not have manes.

9. **True**. Beneath its white fur, the polar bear has black skin that collects heat from the sun and keeps this enormous bear warm.

10. **The gills**. These organs collect oxygen as water moves over them.

11. **False**. Some fish bear live young.

ASTRONOMY

12. **False**. Nothing, not even light, can escape from a black hole.

13. **b. Polaris**. In addition to the North Star, Polaris is also called the northern polestar.

14. **c. Jupiter**. You would weigh more than double your Earth weight on Jupiter.

15. **True**. Earth is actually 93.2 million miles from the Sun.

16. **False**. You would weigh less on the Moon. Multiply your Earth weight by 0.165 to find your Moon weight.

17. **Venus**. Mercury is the closest planet to the Sun.

18. **True**. Scientists believe our galaxy contains at least 200 billion stars.

19. **b. Blue giant**. Blue stars are hotter than yellow or red stars.

20. **True**. The Sun is our solar system's central object.

21. **b. Solar eclipse**. This event happens when the Moon moves between the Earth and the Sun.

EARTH SCIENCE

22. **a. Igneous**. Granite forms when magma cools underground.

23. **False**. It's the opposite. A tributary is a smaller river that flows into a bigger one.

24. **False**. Warm air holds more water vapor than cold air.

25. False. Sunlight only reaches about 3,000 feet below the ocean's surface.

26. b. Mineral.

27. Crust, mantle, core. The crust is the hard, cool outer layer. The mantle is a thick layer of hot rock. The core is the Earth's fiery center.

28. c. Obsidian. The three groups of rocks include sedimentary, metamorphic, and igneous rocks.

29. a. Plain. Raised plains are sometimes called plateaus.

30. Glaciers. These ice sheets cover an estimated 10 to 11% of the Earth's land surface.

31. Lava. Melted rock is called magma beneath the Earth's surface. When magma reaches open air, it is called lava.

32. b. 70%. More than two-thirds of our planet's surface is water.

33. Thermosphere, mesosphere, stratosphere, troposphere. The troposphere is the layer that touches the Earth's surface.

NATURE
34. Apples.

35. False. Cocoa beans originated in South America.

36. False. Elms occur throughout the Northern Hemisphere.

37. c. Taproot. A taproot is the main root of a mature plant.

38. True. An animal may carry seeds on its body or inside its digestive system.

39. b. Deciduous. In the Northern Hemisphere, these trees lose their leaves in the fall and grow new ones in the spring.

40. False. Plants and animals are common in all but the driest areas.

HEALTH
41. Twelve pairs. The total comes to 24 ribs in a typical human.

42. Femur. The largest bone is also called the thigh bone.

43. False. The kidneys are part of the excretory system.

44. a. 206. Together, these bones form the human skeleton.

BRAIN BENDERS
45. True. Pencil "lead" is actually graphite, not the chemical element lead.

46. Red, green, and blue. The primary colors of pigment are red, blue, and yellow.

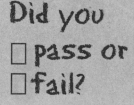

Did you
☐ pass or
☐ fail?

4TH Grade

GROWTH SPURT

In fourth grade, you're not
a little kid anymore. You've learned how
to make connections between facts, and
can figure things out on your own. Your teachers
know how much your brain has grown . . . and they're
eager to keep it growing with more scientific
head scratchers. Are you ready for a challenge?
Answer the questions in this
chapter to find out!

ANIMAL SCIENCE

1. Which of the following is an anthropoid?
   a) Bee
   b) Lobster
   c) Ape

2. There are five main groups of living things. These groups are called:
   a) Species
   b) Genera
   c) Kingdoms

3. As a group, what is the scientific name for animals that lack backbones?

4. Which Greek scientist created the first classification system for living things?

5. Some animals have colors or patterns that help them blend in with the colors of their environment. What is this trait called?

6. When summer ends, large groups of monarch butterflies travel south for the winter. This journey is an example of:
a) Migration
b) Hibernation
c) Vacation

7. **True or False?** You can make a good guess at a fish's age by looking at its scales.

7x7=49 AaBbCcDdEe

8. More than 99% of the mass of our solar system is contained within what heavenly body?

9. Approximately how many years does it take Halley's Comet to make one orbit around the Sun?
   a) 94
   b) 52
   c) 76

Brain Bubble

A Truly Tall Tail

In deep space, comets look like big, dirty snowballs. Near the Sun, however, heat melts some of the "snowball." A light-reflecting cloud of dust and gas called a **coma** forms around the snowball. Some of this matter is pushed backward into a shining tail that can be up to 100 million miles long.

AaBbCcDdEe

10. In 1962, who was the first U.S. astronaut to orbit the Earth?

11. Approximately how long does it take for the Moon to make one full orbit around the Earth?
a) One day
b) One month
c) One year

12. The four main phases of the moon are full moon, first quarter, last quarter, and what?

13. What galaxy is closest in distance to the Milky Way?

7x7=49   AaBbCcDdEe

14. Which four planets in our solar system are known as gas giants?

EARTH SCIENCE

15. Lightning is what type of electricity?
a) Current
b) Alternating
c) Static

16. Sonar uses which of the following to navigate and measure ocean depth?
a) Sound waves
b) Light waves
c) Electromagnetic waves

17. Aurora Borealis is a name for what natural phenomenon?
    a) Northern lights
    b) Southern lights
    c) Solar eclipse

18. The Earth's crust is made of moving plates. Each year, how far do these plates travel?
    a) A few inches
    b) A few yards
    c) A few miles

19. Hardness is a property that helps scientists identify the Earth's minerals. Name the scale that measures this property.

20. In what state is a material's particles spread farthest apart?
    a) Solid
    b) Liquid
    c) Gas

21. When two air masses meet, they form a border called a:

a) Storm

b) Front

c) Squall

22. The Laws of Motion are named for which English scientist who first published his findings in 1687?

NATURE

23. Which of the following trees is considered a conifer?

a) Oak

b) Pine

c) Maple

AaBbCcDdEe

24. Pollen is produced in which part of the flower?
a) Pistil
b) Stamen
c) Pedal

25. What is the name for the process by which plants make their own food?
a) Photosynthesis
b) Oxidation
c) Mitosis

26. What pigment found in plant leaves uses energy from sunlight to make food?

27. True or False? Some plants eat insects.

28. **True or False?** All plants grow from seeds.

29. Coral reefs, tropical rainforests, and deserts are all examples of:
a) Ecologies
b) Ecosystems
c) Biomes

30. **True or False?** Animal bones are the only materials that can turn into fossils.

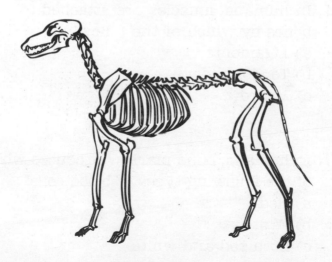

HEALTH

31. Which are blood vessels in the human body?
a) Tibias
b) Cilia
c) Capillaries

32. The hardest tissue in the human body covers the teeth. What is its name?

33. In humans, muscles are attached to bones by which of the following?
a) Ligaments
b) Tendons
c) Marrow

34. In humans, bone marrow produces which of the following types of blood cells?
a) Red
b) White
c) Both red and white

35. The pituitary gland is part of which system in the human body?
a) Circulatory
b) Endocrine
c) Digestive

36. Part of a person's sleep cycle is called the REM cycle. What does REM stand for?

BrainBubble

In Your Dreams

Studies show that our most vivid dreams occur during the REM cycle. Dreams also occur during other periods of sleep, but they are usually gentler. They are also less likely to be remembered.

AaBbCcDdEe

37. How many canine teeth are in a typical adult human mouth?

38. Which blood type is known as the universal recipient?
a) Type A
b) Type O
c) Type AB

39. Human fingernails are primarily made of a protein known as what?
a) Keratin
b) Melanin
c) Calcium

40. The bones called the hammer, the anvil, and the stirrup are located in which part of the human body?

AaBbCcDdEe

7x7=49

Brain Benders

41. In air, an object traveling faster than the speed of sound creates a shock wave. This wave makes a loud sound known as what?

42. What scientist developed the equation $E=MC^2$?

ANIMAL SCIENCE

1. **c. Ape**. The word "anthropoid" means "humanlike."

2. **c. Kingdoms**. The five kingdoms include animals, plants, fungi, protists, and monerans.

3. **Invertebrates**. Animals with backbones are called vertebrates.

4. **Aristotle**. His system was created around 350 BCE and used for more than 2,000 years.

5. **Camouflage**. It helps animals hide in their habitats.

6. **a. Migration**. Many animals migrate with the changing seasons.

7. **True**. Fish scales bear growth rings, just like trees do.

ASTRONOMY

8. **The Sun**. This star is 330,000 times more massive than the Earth.

9. **c. 76**. Halley's Comet is visible from Earth when it nears the Sun.

10. **John Glenn**. He circled the Earth three times in the space capsule *Friendship 7*.

11. **b. One month**. The actual time of the Moon's orbit is 28 days.

12. **New moon**. This phase is also called the dark of the Moon.

13. **The Andromeda galaxy**. It is about 2 million light-years from Earth.

14. **Jupiter, Saturn, Uranus, Neptune**. These planets are the 5th, 6th, 7th, and 8th planets from the Sun.

EARTH SCIENCE

15. **c. Static**. Lightning is a massive static discharge.

16. **a. Sound waves**. The waves bounce off solid objects, creating echoes that can be "read" by computers.

17. **a. Northern lights**. This phenomenon is common in the far northern latitudes.

18. **a. A few inches**. It takes thousands upon thousands of years for plates to make significant progress.

19. **Mohs' Hardness Scale**. It ranks minerals from 1 (softest) to 10 (hardest).

20. **c. Gas**. Materials are least dense in their gas state.

21. **b. Front**. Storms and squalls often occur along a front.

22. **Sir Isaac Newton**. Newton's Laws describe the effects of forces on moving objects.

NATURE

23. **b. Pine**. Pine trees bear cones and needles. Oaks and maples have leaves.

24. **b. Stamen**. The stamen has special sacs that hold the pollen.

25. **a. Photosynthesis**. In this process, plants change light energy into chemical energy.

26. **Chlorophyll**. This green pigment absorbs light energy.

27. **True**. The Venus' flytrap is the most famous carnivorous plant.

28. **False**. Plants can also grow from spores, buds, bulbs, and many other objects.

29. **c. Biomes**. Biomes are composed of many smaller ecosystems.

30. **False**. Wood, shells, leaves, animal tracks, burrows, and even dung have been fossilized.

HEALTH
31. **c. Capillaries**. Tibias are leg bones. Cilia are small hairs.

32. **Enamel**. It occurs in many animals, not just humans.

33. **b. Tendons**. Ligaments join bones to bones. Marrow is a substance found inside bones.

34. **c. Both red and white**. New supplies of these cells are constantly produced by the marrow.

35. **b. Endocrine**. The pituitary gland produces and releases many important hormones.

36. **Rapid Eye Movement**. As the name suggests, a sleeper's eyeballs move back and forth quickly during this period.

37. **Four**. Strong and pointed, the canine teeth hold and tear food.

38. **c. Type AB**. A person with this blood type can receive blood of any other type.

39. **a. Keratin**. Human hair is also made of keratin.

40. **The middle ear**. These tiny bones are found between the outer ear and the inner ear.

BRAIN BENDERS
41. **Sonic boom**. Aircraft that travel faster than sound are called supersonic.

42. **Albert Einstein**. This German-born scientist is best known for his theory of relativity.

Did you
☐ pass or
☐ fail?

5TH Grade

TOP OF THE HEAP

Fifth grade is the top of the heap, at least as far as elementary school is concerned. Will you ace the test? Or, like those grown-up students on TV, will you flunk out? Here's your final exam!

64

ANIMAL SCIENCE

1. **True or False?** Insects are responsible for pollinating many plants.

2. Different kinds of animals sometimes live closely together for their entire lives. These long-term relationships are called:
a) Symbiosis
b) Proximity
c) Cohabitation

ASTRONOMY

3. Halley's Comet is named after an English astronomer. What is his name?

4. How many astronauts were onboard each space capsule launched during NASA's Gemini Space Program?
a) One
b) Two
c) Four

5. What is the most abundant element in the universe?

6. The Earth spins on its axis. In scientific terms, this spin is called:
   a) Revolution
   b) Rotation
   c) Orbit

7. At its closest, the Moon is roughly how far away from the Earth?
   a) 22,500 miles
   b) 225,000 miles
   c) 2,250,000 miles

8. The Sun's energy reaches the Earth in two primary forms. Name these forms.

9. What is the scientific name for a star's brightness?

HEALTH

10. In the human body, the adrenal glands are located directly above what organ?

11. **True or False?** Scientist Gregor Mendel is best known for his work in the field of physics.

12. What Scottish scientist discovered penicillin in 1928?

Brain Bubble

Bacteria Beware

Penicillin was the first drug in the **antibiotic** family. Antibiotics slow the growth of certain bacteria, or destroy the bacteria altogether. They are therefore vitally important in the treatment of bacterial diseases such as tetanus, scarlet fever, and tuberculosis.

13. In the 1950s, Dr. Jonas Salk discovered a vaccine that would protect people from what disease?

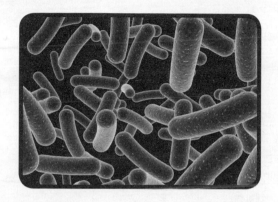

14. Which of these structures is not found inside a human cell?
a) Chromosome
b) Mitochondria
c) Chloroplast

15. True or False? Human blood is considered a tissue.

16. In what part of the human body are the alveoli found?

AaBbCcDdEe

17. When you kick a ball, you move your leg using what type of muscle?
a) Smooth
b) Voluntary
c) Cardiac

18. By weight, water makes up about what percentage of the human body?
a) 10-20%
b) 40-50%
c) 60-70%

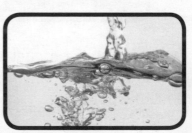

EARTH SCIENCE

19. Which element comprises the majority of the Earth's atmosphere?

7x7=49   AaBbccDdEe

20. What is the name of the scientist usually credited with creating the Periodic Table?

21. Name the geologic era we are living in.

BrainBubble

Bye-Bye, Dinosaurs

An event called a **mass extinction** marked the end of the Mesozoic Era and the beginning of the Cenozoic. During this event, many plants and animals disappeared, including all dinosaurs. Many scientists think that a comet or asteroid strike caused this massive extinction.

22. By definition, an anemometer measures the speed of what?

23. In which biome is the average air temperature likely to be highest?
a) Rainforest
b) Tundra
c) Taiga

24. Estuaries usually contain what type of water?
a) Fresh
b) Salty
c) Brackish

25. Collectively, what is the name of the natural processes that break rock into soil, sand, and other particles?

26. What precious metal has the symbol "Ag" on the Periodic Table of the Elements?

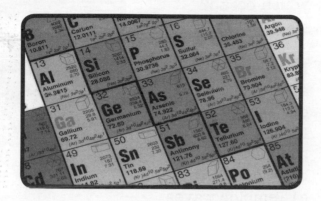

27. At room temperature, approximately 70 degrees Fahrenheit, two elements on the Periodic Table exist in a liquid state. Bromine is one of them.
Name the other.

28. After discovering radium in 1898, which French chemist became the first woman to win a Nobel Prize?

AaBbCcDdEe

29. A group of volcanoes called the "Ring of Fire" surrounds which ocean?

30. In scientific terms, an earthquake sends out energy in the form of:
a) Shaker waves
b) Seismic waves
c) Temblor waves

31. Most scientists believe that the Earth's land masses were once joined together in one "supercontinent." What is the name of this supercontinent?

32. True or False? Most of the Earth's weather occurs in the mesosphere.

7x7=49 AaBbCcDdEe

33. In the ocean, underwater earthquakes sometimes create enormous waves. What are these waves called?

NATURE

34. What do plants lose in the process known as transpiration?
a) Roots
b) Water vapor
c) Seeds

35. Materials lose all of their heat energy at -459.67 degrees Fahrenheit. What is the scientific name for this point?

36. True or False? The Law of Conservation of Matter states that matter is not created, destroyed, or altered during a physical or chemical change.

37. Cell membranes allow water to pass through while blocking dissolved substances. What is this process called?

38. Plants grow toward light sources. This response is called:
a) Photoreaction
b) Phototropism
c) Photosynthesis

39. Which of these objects is not a seed?
a) Corn kernel
b) Lima bean
c) Acorn

40. When charcoal burns, carbon reacts with oxygen to produce carbon dioxide. This is an example of a:
a) Physical change
b) Chemical change
c) Reactive change

7x7=49   AaBbCcDdEe

Brain Benders

41. Two bicyclists are traveling in opposite directions at precisely 20 miles per hour. These cyclists have the same:

a) Speed

b) Velocity

c) Both A and B

42. Density describes the mass of an object divided by what?

ANIMAL SCIENCE

1. **True**. Insects and some other animals carry pollen from one flower to another as they move around.

2. **a. Symbiosis**. Animals in a symbiotic relationship usually — but not always — help each other in some way.

ASTRONOMY

3. **Edmond Halley**. In 1705, he first described the comet that now bears his name.

4. **b. Two**. Each of the 10 manned Gemini missions included a command pilot and a backup pilot.

5. **Hydrogen**. This element makes up about 75% of the universe's mass.

6. **b. Rotation**. One full rotation equals one day.

7. **b. 225,000 miles**. At its farthest, the distance increases to about 252,000 miles.

8. **Light and heat**. These energy forms stream outward from the Sun in all directions.

9. **Magnitude**. There are two types of magnitude: absolute magnitude, or how bright the star really is, and apparent magnitude, or how bright it looks from a fixed distance.

HEALTH

10. **The kidneys**. The adrenal glands actually sit right on the kidneys.

11. **False**. Gregor Mendel is known for his work in genetics.

12. **Alexander Fleming**. He earned the Nobel Prize for his discovery.

13. **Polio**. Thanks to Salk's vaccine, polio has been eradicated in all but four countries.

14. **c. Chloroplast**. This organelle is found only in plant cells.

15. **True**. Blood is a connective tissue.

16. **The lungs**. The alveoli are tiny air sacs. They release carbon dioxide into the lungs and collect fresh oxygen.

17. **b. Voluntary**. These muscles are also called striated muscles.

18. **c. 60-70%**. All humans need lots of water to survive.

EARTH SCIENCE

19. **Nitrogen**. This gas makes up more than 78% of our atmosphere.

20. **Dmitri Mendeleev**. This Russian chemist organized all then-known elements into the modern format in 1869.

21. **The Cenozoic Era**. This era started 65.5 million years ago and continues to present day.

22. **Wind**. The anemometer is a basic meteorological tool.

23. **a. Rainforest**. Rainforests are found in the hot tropics. Tundra and taiga are found in the far north.

24. **c. Brackish**. Brackish water is a mixture of salty and fresh water.

25. **Weathering**. Water and wind are two main causes of weathering.

26. **Silver**. The symbol "Ag" comes from the Latin word *argentum*, which means "shining."

27. **Mercury**. This element is liquid between temperatures of about -40 to 674 degrees Fahrenheit.

28. **Marie Curie**. She received two Nobel Prizes, one in 1903 and one in 1911.

29. **The Pacific Ocean**. The Ring of Fire is a long chain of volcanoes found along the edges of the Pacific plate.

30. **b. Seismic waves**. These waves spread outward from the earthquake's center like ripples on a pond.

31. **Pangaea or Pangea**. This name comes from Greek words meaning "entire earth."

32. **False**. Nearly all of our planet's weather occurs in the troposphere, the atmosphere's lowest layer.

33. **Tsunamis**. When they reach the shore, tsunamis can be over 80 feet tall.

NATURE

34. **b. Water vapor**. Transpiration occurs when water evaporates from a plant's open-air parts.

35. **Absolute zero**. It is sometimes expressed as 0 degrees Kelvin.

36. **False**. Matter is not created or destroyed during these changes, but it can be altered.

37. **Osmosis**. Cells get most of their water by osmosis.

38. **b. Phototropism**. It is caused by chemicals in a plant's stem.

39. **c. Acorn**. An acorn contains seeds, but it is not a seed itself. It is technically a fruit.

40. **b. Chemical change**. By definition, chemical changes produce one or more new substances. They are also known as reactions.

BRAIN BENDERS

41. **a. Speed**. Velocity refers not only to speed but to direction as well.

42. **Volume**. The formula is written as $D = M/V$.

Did you
☐ pass or
☐ fail?

SCHOOL'S OUT!

How did you do? Even if you didn't get every question right, real life isn't like the TV show. You don't flunk out because of a wrong answer. You get the chance to try again — and trying again is how you learn.

Go back to any questions that gave you trouble. Study the correct answers until you know them by heart. Before long, you'll be a science whiz. More important, you'll be able to say the line that many adults haven't been able to say in Mr. Foxworthy's TV classroom:

"Yes, I AM smarter than a 5th grader!"